Table of contents

I0505447

INTRODUCTION

Today in this area I'll teach you everything related to email marketing now this is a very special Time because in this Time I'll be covering everything that you need to know about email marketing first of all we'll be using only free resources secondly I'll be covering some really amazing things that most of you guys might not have seen before for example

I'll show you how to run an automation campaign now let me give you an example of automation campaign so in this campaign what happens is you can send a welcome message or welcome email whenever someone joins your newsletter

so you don't have to do anything manually you don't have to type anything manually every time someone joins the newsletter you can simply automate that we'll also see how to do a/b testing of the newsletter I'll explain you more about a/b testing later on in this Time we will also see ecommerce related things like automatically sending thank you message to first-time customer or maybe sending coupons to first-time customer so that it motivates them to purchase again abundant cart follow-up and many more ecommerce related emails are also included in this particular book

we'll also see how to create newsletter for manned pop-ups to attract and collect more emails and let me remind you again that all these things are absolutely free now because this Time is quite long you can jump to different sections by clicking on different time frames which is given in the Time description below now before proceeding further

I would like to recommend you guys to implement the things if you find this Time helpful give a thumbs up if you have any doubt throughout the Time if it did not understand anything or maybe if you have some requests some suggestions for me you can leave them in the comment section below now without wasting any more time let's get started.

E-mail Marketing

First of all you need to come this website **mailchimp.com** so simply type in MailChimp calm in the URL bar and you have to login if you don't already have an account simply click on signup or click   on

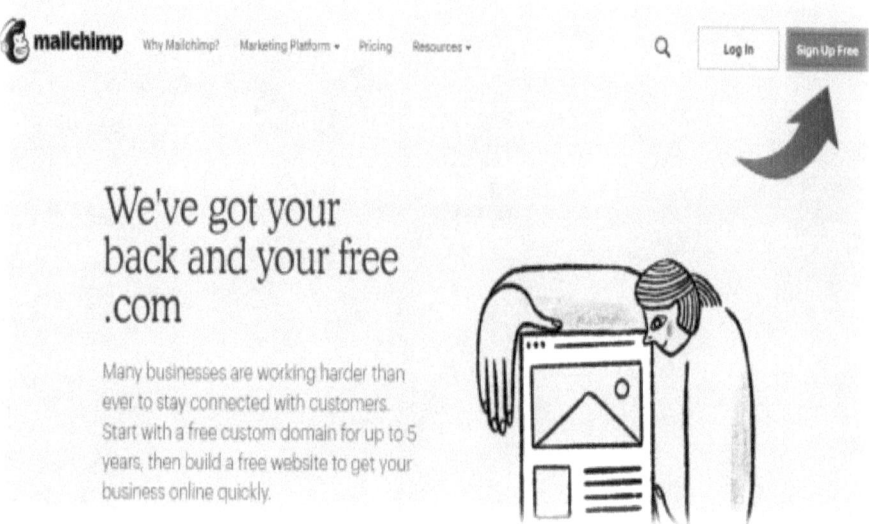

this create an account now you simply have to enter your e-mail address so let me do that choose a username whatever you like so let me choose this username and let's choose a password

so I'm choosing this password now click on get started now as you can   see   they   say   that   they   have   sent   a

Welcome to Mailchimp

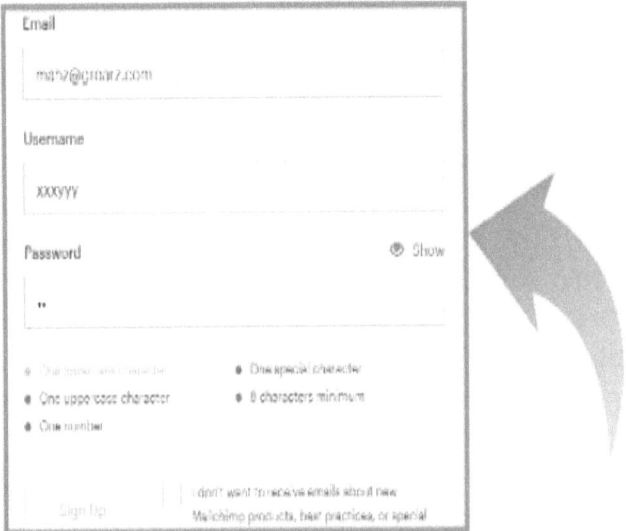

message to whatever email address you have put in the last step and you have to click on the link to activate your account so let's do that go to your email provider whatever email product you're using you get this mail as you can see now we need to click on this activate account button and this will activate our MailChimp account now we need to click on this button I'm not a robot alright now let's enter the first name and last name so enter your first name last name over here click on continue what is the name of your business so my business name is technewser and do you have a website a yeah I do have a website but what I'll do is I'll enter this website technewser in okay

so let me enter that website click on continue enter your address for you all right so once you enter your address simply click on continue do you have a list of email subscribers now I want to show you everything from scratch so I'll select no whether you have it you don't have it just select no we want to start everything fresh everything from scratch so, I'm selecting no and click on continue you can connect your social media links you can simply click on this plus button connect your Facebook account and Twitter account we are not doing that right now

so I'll click on continue now we don't need to do this so just click on no right now okay and this is just a newsletter thing so I don't want this so I won't take on that and I'll just click on this button I guess now as you can see within a minute we have created and we have our active MailChimp account now what we need to do is we need to start creating lists so let me cut this thing now click on this audience which is at the top and you'll see this manage audience click on that click on view audience

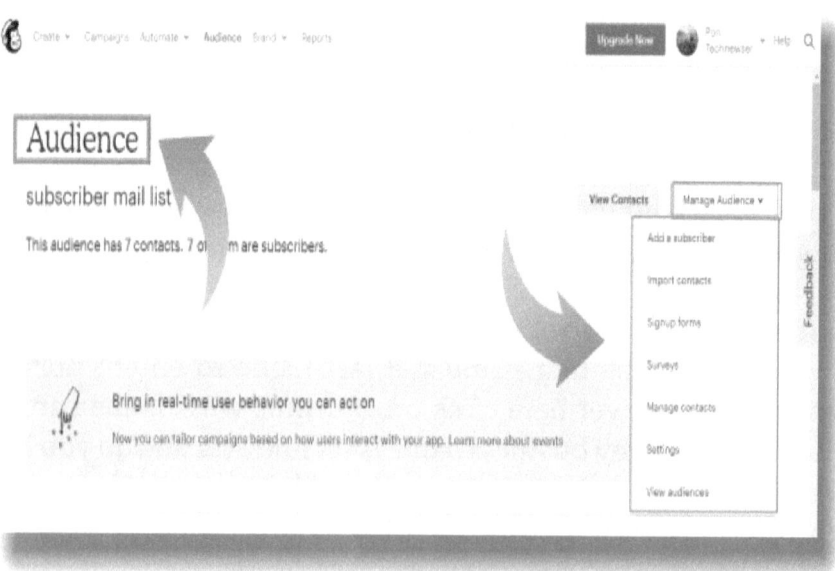

now we need to create this audience one audience or one list is automatically created by the name of your company so I selected my company name technewser and the one subscriber is your own email address okay now if you want to create a new list you can click on create audience and you can also click on this link create audience now creating lists is very important for example if you if you just want one single MailChimp account to handle different email addresses or different newsletter sections for example suppose I have a website block to comm and I am doing email marketing now I am doing two three types of **email marketing** like I want to send you know newsletter related to affiliate marketing I want to send newsletter related to **growing on YouTube** I want to send newsletter related to SEO so obviously all the audiences will be different so I'll use different

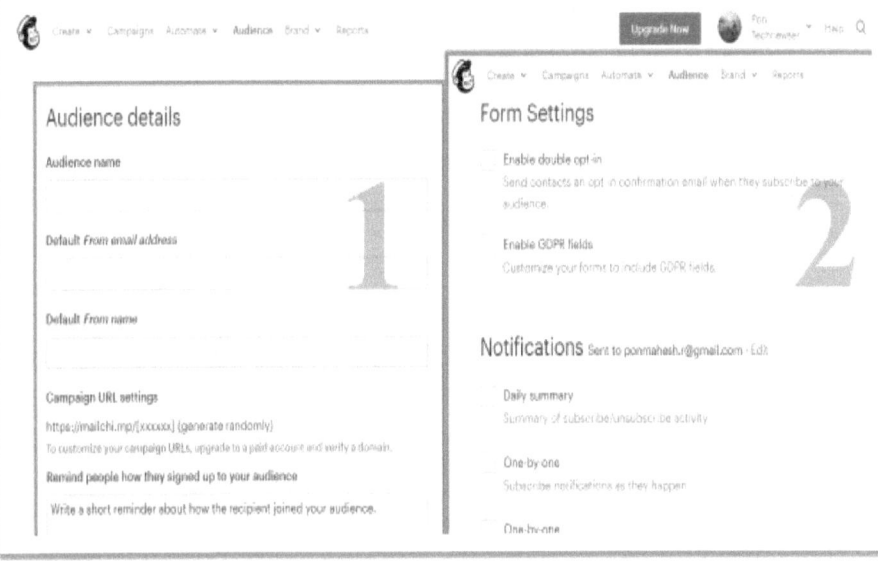

different lists and I'll send different things to all different lists okay if you don't understand that don't worry when we start creating everything when we go further when we start campaigning when we create template and everything you'll understand it much better in simple words you can understand right now that you have to create different audience

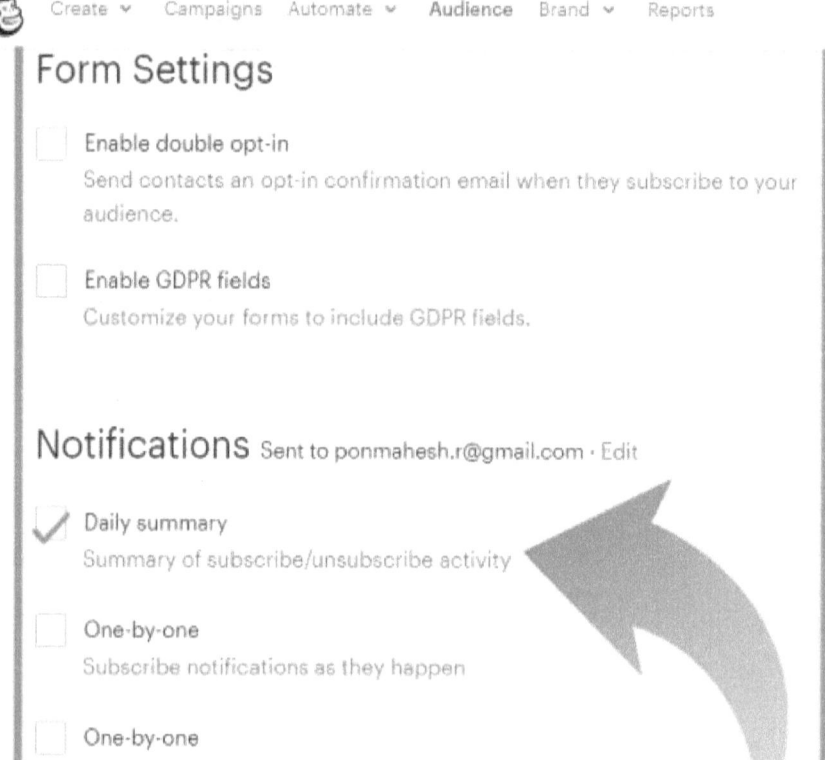

which you want to target for different things okay now in audience name whatever you enter or your that will be visible by the customer so make sure you put something good or with your so I'll just type in a Technewser email marketing newsletter so suppose this audience or this list which I'm creating is for email marketing

so whoever is you know signing up on my newsletter who wants to learn email marketing this is for them okay email marketing newsletter now from email address so you can simply enter your email address like New York or New Year at gmail.com or near at yahoo.com whatever your email addresses or if you have the better option is to enter a business email for example mahz@groarz.com something like that okay which has your website as the extension so that is called a **business email** if you don't know how to create a business email there is a link or there is a Time on my channel you can watch that Time and you can create it for free now under default from name just type in the From me name that should be shown to the person

so whenever a person receives a meal they will see that this is from this particular person now after that your company name your address and everything should be over here now you have few options forms a enable double opt-in if you select this thing if you enable double a double opt-in

which I don't recommend or sometimes it is recommended laughs it all depends on you the type of settings that you want if you enable this thing so whenever someone enters their email address under your you know newsletter form they will have to verify their email address like they will get a code on the email address they will click on activate account and after that they will be added to the list

if you don't antique this so whenever someone comes to your website they enter the email address in your newsletter form they will be added to the list okay so that is what it is now how do you want to receive notification if you select daily summary that your options daily summaries **subscribe and unsubscribe**

if you select this a one by one subscribe and unsubscribe so suppose one person has subscribed I'll get a notification one person another person subscribed after five minutes I'll get another notification so in one day if 100 people are subscribing to my mail I'll get hundred notifications okay so that is what it is what I recommend is is to select this one daily summary so that every day you will get one mail and in that you have this summary of how many people subscribe and unsubscribe today okay

so select this much click on save okay it says please check your entry and try again so we just left this thing remind people how they signed up to your audience so you have to remind people how did they are why are they receiving this thing how did they sign up so as you can see there is an example given at the bottom you are receiving this mail because you opted in at our website so let's do the same thing well I guess as you can see I have typed in the same thing you are receiving this mail because you opted in at our website block to calm so you can type in something like that and go at the bottom click on save alright so with this we have completed or we have created our list okay so we have created a new list now similarly you can create different lists for for different target audiences so you have seen this you can create n number of lists now okay now what I want to do is I want to create a template so template is basically the design that you will be sending to the person whoever is receiving the email

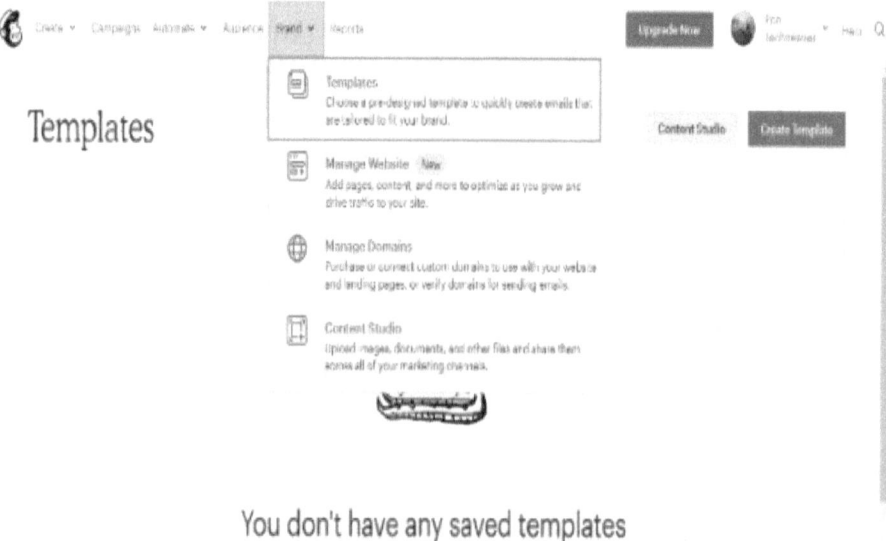

You don't have any saved templates

A template is a saved design that can be reused when creating email campaigns.

so let's see you will see that template you will understand what we are talking about so to create a template at the top you'll see this option **templates** click on that I guess it says you don't have any templates you need to create one new so we have this button over here create template click on that now there are few options for example you can select a layout and start designing the template you can select a theme which is a pre-built theme you can simply select any theme just change the content and you can use that or you can code your own

so you get if you want you can use **HTML CSS** to code your own template now if you want to use a theme you can click on themes and whatever you like it for example if you like the first one if you want to see how it looks you can click on this search I can click on that alright as you can see this is how it will look it has this this is your logo this is your site name or your company name there is a background then you have some text

Then we have some person meter artists some call-to-action links like read more this is the call to action and we have some more things over here so if you want you can simply use this let me cut this thing if you want you can use this you can simply replace whatever content is present you can replace they that with your own content what you can do you can use the layout

so I generally use layouts that that is more better for me for example and there there are few layouts which I use quite often for example make announcement or tell a story and educate these three are very useful for me okay

so I am for example let's use the educate one in this so I'll click on this educate and this will use this layout now we have to redesign this layout however you like it you can change everything you can replace everything and create your own unique design now as you can see at the top we have to enter our logo so if you want to enter y'all over simply click on that you'll get this option at the right-hand side click on replace to replace this image with your own logo image so let me upload my logo so maybe let me use this one I'll click on this open now this is a white logo okay so I'll click on   insert

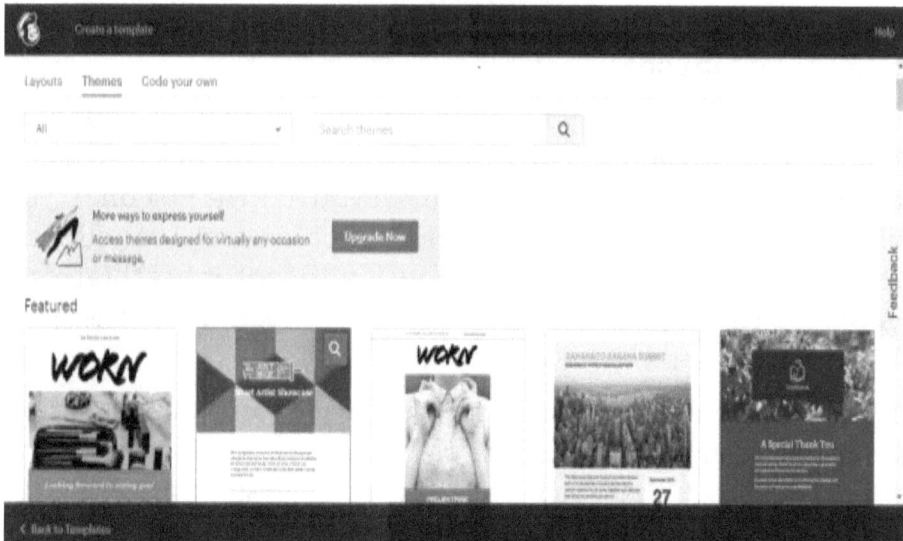

as you can see I cannot see the white logo because the background is also a little bit like white so I'll change the background color to do that I will click on this color I will select some color now as you can see you can see the logo so you can change the background color as well okay just like this so I think blue is looking fine if you want you can enter some image in the background for example let's upload some image let's upload this one select this click on insert now as you can see there is an image in the background so you can use an image in the background or you can also use a color so

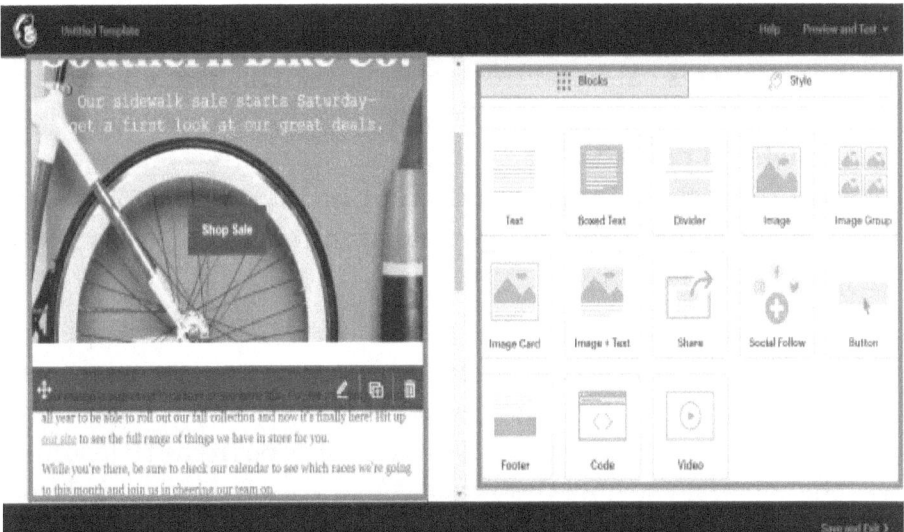

whatever you like it so maybe I want the image in the background and I want to change the logo now because white logo is not looking good so I'll click on this pencil button click on replace and let me upload a colourful **logo** like this one click on open select this click on insert ok now as you can see this is a logo this is the background

so this is how you do it now after that we have this thing so I I'll do one thing I'll click on it and I'll change the text so maybe oh you have to decide why you're creating this template so maybe I am creating this template or to inform people about the latest post that I have written or published on my website okay so maybe latest - or latest 3 posts that I have published

so that is what I am doing with you so instead of help people use your product or service I'll select this much I'll delete it and I'll enter my link or my text or your latest post from block - calm okay so this is how we'll do it as you can see using layout saves you a lot of time you don't have to design anything you simply have to replace the content now instead of this thing this dummy text delete it and type in something like this the following post are the latest post which are published on my website whatever you like it okay you can type in that thing right so I have typed in that text now I don't want this button

I don't want this call to action so I'll hover this and I'll click on this dustbin I clean this will delete this block click on delete okay that is deleted now instead of all these three things I want to upload my the featured image of my blog and the title so I'll select the first one replace this image upload my own image let me do that let me upload three images

so I'll upload let me see maybe this this and this click on open alright so all three images are uploaded first I want to use this one so I'll select this click on insert now as you can see this image is now present so instead of choosier approach I'll type in the title which was the this was the hotel booking website books I'll type in hotel booking book ok now I'll change this text and type in watch this Time though if you want to create a hotel booking website all right so similarly I'll click on second one and I will replace the image so I'll click on replace I'll use the DB image select this DB click

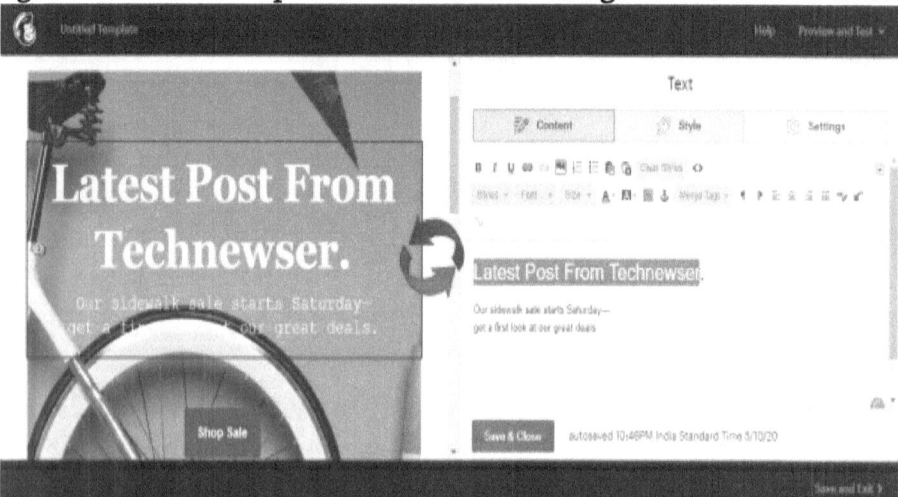

on insert okay now instead of this title share one idea at a time I'll type in DB book and instead of this text I'll type in watch the db2 - obviously I'm not doing this for real I'm just typing in something you basically have to replace everything every dummy content so nothing dummy content should be left on the website for example this photo is a dummy content this line one last thing should be replaced this takes this is a good spot to share additional resources this text every text or dummy text or image is present over here that should be replaced okay

so I'm just typing in watch the DVD book now click on save and close now obviously you should remember one thing whenever when I am trying to give this link to my DVD tool or my hotel booking tutor so I should link this with something

so I'm link I'm I'll select this image I'll click on link and I will go to my website for example this was the one so I'll right-click on this click on copy link address and I'll paste it over here okay so you should link that so whenever someone clicks on that they should be redirected to that if you want to link this title hotel booking book you can select this much and you can click on this pin button this will link it so select that paste in the link wherever you want to link it

click on insert link okay now as you can see that is turned into a link so make sure to do that okay or else it will just be simple image and text there won't be any links now I am I'm just deleting the third one so I will delete it and this text I'll just change it and I'll type in thank you and I will delete this text and I'll type in let me know if you have anything to ask all right so

we have changed everything now we have these social links at the bottom this is the footer click on those social links and you have your Facebook Twitter and all this link so I will type in my Facebook link okay you simply have to change your Facebook link copy and paste in your Facebook link that Twitter link Instagram I'm not on Instagram but I'll add some different link for different person and website and instead of **mailchimp.com** I'll type in **groarz.com**

click on save and close now these things at the bottom when you click on that as you can see copyright instead of this current here whatever the current here is that will show for example copyright 2020 instead of this code it will show your company name all rights reserved so all these texts are present simply click on save and close

so we have this design ready now we can click on save and exit you can name this template anything for example I will name it latest blocks click on save now again and again we don't have to create new templates what we can do is we have saved this as a template now we can use this template later on

we can design it differently and we can send it so that will save some time because you don't have to put in the logo and everything we just have to replace the content ok so with this we have also created the template now I think it's time to integrate MailChimp with our website so for example I want to integrate MailChimp with this website block 2.5 m dot in so whatever website you want to integrate this with you can go to your website go to your dashboard if you don't know how to go to your dashboard you simply enter your website name forward slash **WP - admin** now

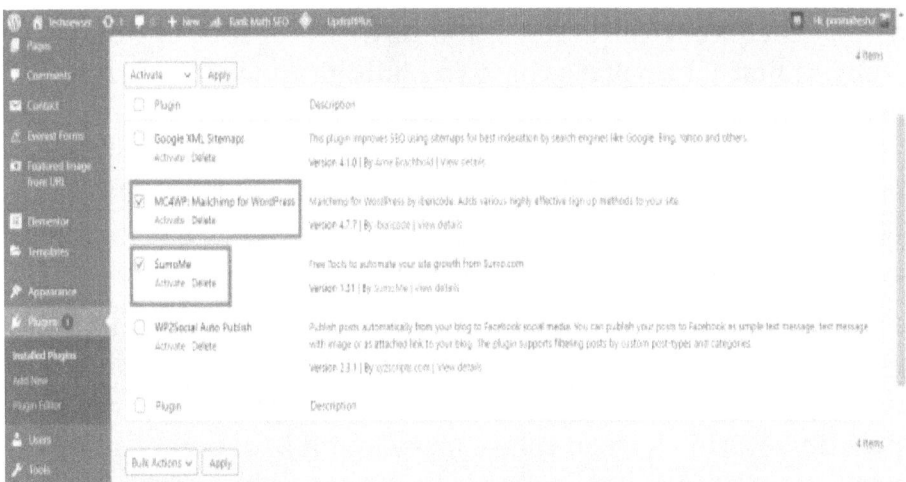

we need to install few plugins ok so i'll how our plugins click on add new i'll install two three plugins over here first of all I'll install I'll just type in MailChimp and I'll get few recommendations so I'll install this one MailChimp for WordPress click on install then after that will you will also install this one mail stream for WooCommerce install this so this MailChimp for WordPress is by I berry code MailChimp for **WooCommerce** is by MailChimp.

so install both this now don't activate it right now we need one more plugin so type in under search bar type in sumo now this is the one sumo boost conversion and sales click on install now these plugins will enable us to add different forms and pop-ups on our website we'll see that things are later on okay now click on install plugins now it's time to activate all these three plugins okay

so I'll tick mark this or maybe whatever plug-in you want to select for example I want to select this this and this these three plugins that we have just installed so I'll select bulk action and click on activate click on apply okay as you can see oh yo I got an error a two plugins were activated the third one did not activate it because the I don't have you commerce on this website okay so if you're using the **MailChimp** for WooCommerce make sure you have who commerce on your website

so I'll untick this maelstrom for who commerce I'll use this on some other website I'll show you how to use that but on other website first I'll activate these to MailChimp for WordPress and sumo means so I'll take mark these two and click on apply alright so both are applied now I need to I'll get this option MailChimp for WP at the left hand side how are that and click on MailChimp now over here you have to enter your API key okay so what I'll do is I'll come over here now from here

if you want to get your API key click on this click on account now click on extra you'll see API keys option click on that now scroll down you don't have any active API key but it's fine you can simply click on this button create a key and it will create a key for you instantly now as you can see this is the key copy this API key come over here and paste in this key click on Save Changes alright now as you can see it says connected so this website is now connected with our **MailChimp account**

And after that as you can see at the bottom it will get all your list so we have created one list and there is one list which is automatically present so we have two lists as you can see blog block code which was automatically present and blocked with email marketing newsletter which we created now this one does not have any subscriber but this one has one subscriber so we have both the list

which means that we have successfully integrated our website with MailChimp now let's integrate soon plug in with the MailChimp so you'll see this zoom option at the bottom however that and click on dashboard now you'll get this option we need to do one thing we need to connect this thing so I'll click on Summa settings okay so I I see over here that this is automatically connected but if it is not connected simply do the same thing or just enter your email address and and create up new account

if you don't have an account with Sumo already you can just enter your email address and password and it will create an account for you so it's quite easy I think my website is already connected so I am NOT getting that option ok so we have successfully integrated our website with MailChimp now let me show you how we can create different forms that you can put different newsletter forms that you can put in to add different places on your website to collect email addresses

For example: if you see this website this is by the way if you want if you see this complete design this is part of my latest book if you go to my channel you will see this **how to start a money-making blog** for free so I recently created this Time how to start a money-making blog for free so I created I showed people how you can create our complete blog using all free resources like free theme free plugin free page builder everything is free and this has email marketing of capabilities email marketing **affiliate marketing** then you also have google adsense and everything guest post option is also available

so if you want to create your blog for free if you want to DS redesign your blog make sure to watch our YouTube channel if you need that link it will be provided on the end of the book. how to start money-making block for free ok very important so in that book I have shown people how to create this design so this form that you see over here this is the form that we need to create on our website so that people can come over here they can enter their name email address click on sign up when they click on sign up they will be added on our list and we can use that list to do email marketing or to send newsletters so let's see how we can do that so for that I'll come over here I'll cover this **MailChimp 4wp** and click on form now let's create a new form if you see by default there will be one form already created for you

now I am using the ocean WP theme if you are using some different theme at this page this section will look some you friend because this plugin the great thing about this plugin is that it uses the theme design it does not create another design it uses the team design to design this particular form okay so I already have this design as you can see the name email address and signup button

so I don't need to do any changes if you need to do some changes for example if you don't need this name this is the code for name as you can see the thing that I have marked you can select this much click on delete that name thing is gone now you have only email address okay control-z because I want that thing

so this is the form now if you want you can simply first of all go to our Save Changes now you have this link over here you have this shortcode over here you simply have to copy this clear select this thing it will select everything right click click on copy now wherever you want to enter this wherever you want to put this or show this thing show this form you can paste in this code and it will start showing for example let me open the home page as you can see it is already showing on my home page but what I want to do is I want to do one thing I will click on edit with Elementor because I'm using element or whatever you are using del does not matter whether you using TV visual visual composer or element or that does not matter

we simply have to copy this code this short code on and paste in wherever you want to show it so let's see so let me delete this okay now that is gone now if I want to show that form I can use this text editor okay now I'll delete everything and just paste in this code okay click on update let's see how it looks click on this preview changes button now as you can see that is showing on my website now if I want to show this on somewhere else

For example if I want to show this at the bottom of this page I'll click on this plus button single row text editor drag and drop paste in this shortcode click on update come over here refresh this page now let's scroll down now as you can see when we scroll down we have this form so wherever you want to use this form you can simply paste in that code on that Page okay

so let's cut this thing now when you use this thing MailChimp 4wp you also get a plug-in you also get a widget which you can use to show for example let me show you let's open this single post now as you can see this has this sidebar so whenever you want to show that thing a newsletter thing in the sidebar you can use that widget let me show you how we can do that so if you want to use that with that widget you can how our appearance and click on widgets okay now you'll see this option MailChimp sign up form select this wherever you want to for example default I want to enter or show this on default sidebar select that click on add widget ok whatever title you want

so title is newsletter fine click on done come over here refresh this page now as you can see this newsletter the form that we created is also displayed at the sidebar so it will display at this sidebar of every single post ok now whenever someone enters the email at name and email address they will be signed up to the list which you have selected now if you want to change the list you can come over here and you can also always do this setting click on mail stream for WB and under that you'll see this form click on form now here you have this settings click on settings and you have to list sir this form subscribe to wherever you want for example I want to whenever someone clicks on or enters the email address and click on sign up I want them to be entered or to be included in this list Technewser email marketing newsletter okay so select that click on Save Changes now when you come over here when you click on audience let's see what happens as you can see this audience or this list Technewser email marketing has zero contacts now let me do one thing let me come over here refresh this page and let me enter my name near my email address ponmahesh.r@gmail.com and click on sign up now let's come over here refresh this page alright I see that that is not added over here because as you can see here it says thank you signup request was successful

please check your email inbox so here that double opt-in thing is going on that setting is going on I need to disable that so for that I'll come back to this setting and you as you can see who your double opt-in is enabled I'll select this no and click on Save Changes okay let's try it again enter the name email address click on sign up ok now as you can see it says given email address is already subscribed thank you now let's check it again let's refresh this page now as you can see it has one contact

so this is working now if you want to show this form this form even on some post or page you can do that as well for example you can come over here how our post click on add new let's add a new post and enter this thing over there or maybe let's not add a new post let's do one thing for example in this post only I if I want to add this form I'll click on edit post ok now

wherever I want to add it for example if I want to add this between these two texts I'll click on this plus button I'll search for shortcode ok and pasting that shortcode ok this one **MailChimp shortcode** click on update now let's view this post so I'll you will see this view post link right click on this open that in a new tab let's see now as you can see between these two things now this form is showing so as you can see you can show this form anywhere you want okay using this shortcode

so this is working fine for us now let's create pop-ups and smart bar I can see that smart bar is already present as you can see at the top this is the smart bar but I because I said you earlier that I think that this is already linked with sumo but if you don't see that smart bar if you want to create a pop-up let me show you how we can do that again come back to your dashboard now click on sumo from the left hand side so click on sumo all right now you need to click on my apps now when you do that it will open a new tab for you and you will see this sumo me.com site and you have this dashboard over here now we need to create a new pop-up and we need to create a new smart bar

so let's do that for that you will click on forms at the top and as you can see I have created these two let me delete them so that I can show you from scratch how to create this let me delete this as well ok now both are deleted now let us create an so I'll click on create new form and I want to create this thing this is a pop-up so whenever someone you have seen these things many times now this is everything everything over here is free now you should at the left hand side you'll see all the options related to this pop-up okay so what is the goal of creating this pop-up is it collecting emails or adding call-to-action or getting social shares okay as you can see if you want more followers on Twitter more likes on Facebook or is to whether it is to get a call back or call to action whatever the aim is you can select that for example our goal over here is to collect more emails so I'll select the first one now forum type is the second option click on that whether you want pop up smart box or inline form click trigger pop up whatever type of a pop-up you want so we want this simple pop-up okay I'll select the first one after that we have this third one which is the design

so in the free version only the default design which is this one is present if you want to use some other design like this you have to upgrade your account now that is not required because this is quite expensive I guess it is $40 per month I think that is quite expensive so it is not needed just make sure default is selected then after that a visibility when should this pop-up display on your website so there if you select this smart mode that is what I recommend so in smart mode what happens is when a person tries to leave your website for example I'm suppose I am visiting this website when I try to leave my work leave this website for which means that when I try to bring my cursor to close this tab that pop-up will display okay so that is what smart mode is again let me explain you

I'm reading this post if I want to close this tab I will no bring my cursor at the top of the tab to close the tab at that time that pop-up will display before I enter or before I exit this website or if you want to display at a manual mode you can select this manual mode now we have a lot of option for example if the visitor has seen a pop-up in one it has not seen a pop-up in one our one minute one month show it okay or maybe in time if you see after five seconds or so whatever option you want to show you can just select that from here I would recommend you to select this smart mode now under success if you want to redirect them to some different page once they have entered their email address you can do that as well I think not required so we'll leave that now the second a sixth option last option is to connect to email service now we want to connect this to MailChimp now as you can see for me it is already connected

but no worries I'll click on connect and I will disconnect this okay just to show you guys how to connect it now as you can see that is disconnected now again click on connect click on connect it will open this new tab for me enter your user name and password click on login it will automatically connect **MailChimp** with your website now as you can see this is connected let's click on save so this thing is now active now click on publish so once you click on publish as you can see one post is created now whenever someone visits your website for example let me refresh this page and let's see whether that pop-up is showing or not now as you can see it is not showing where whether I scroll down

whether I scroll up but when I try to exit this page let me show you okay I am NOT getting that pop-up so let me do one thing let me open this website in a new incognito window and let's try it again alright let's try it again okay so let me try to exit this page now as you can see when I tried to exit this page I got this pop-up okay when I try to bring my cursor to close this tab I get this pop-up okay so this is working fine let me cut this thing now let's see how we can add smart bar or obviously if you want you can add some different type of forms so click on create new form again our goal is to collect emails second type form type I want a smart bar okay this is the one so this is smart bar this will be us this will stick at the top or bottom wherever you want to stick this thing okay or you can change these text like instead of submit form a closed pop-up whatever you want to say you can change these things if you want to change the background color you can change that as well so you can design it accordingly now visibility again make sure smart mode is selected success what happens when their same options okay as you can see it is already connected because we have connected the previous form so this is already connected so let's click on publish now you should see two options

so here let me again open this in a new incognito window alright as you can see now it is not showing but when I scroll down and when I try to scroll up now as you can see both the options are showing now the pop-up is also displaying and this smart tab or the smart bar is also displaying at the top so these things are working so let me cut these things or I guess so with this most of the basic things are done we have created a list we have created a template we have seen how to integrate MailChimp with our website we have created pop-ups we have created newsletter forms and we have also created a smart part now comes the most important thing running campaigns and that different types of campaigns which I have explained you or which I have mentioned about in the introduction of this Timethat is automation that is a be testing that is regular there is plain text everything is present I'll show you all the four types okay so to do that to run campaigns you have to simply click on first of all you have to come to MailChimp and click on campaigns which is at the top or I guess now I click on create campaign and I will select email okay I always select this email so select this now there are 4 types of campaigns regular automated plaintext and AB test okay let me start with plain text because that is the most simple one so I will select that you can give a name to this campaign so I will just name it plain text click on begin alright now you have to choose the audience or to which you want to target so I'll target this audience **Technewser email marketing** newsletter now do you want to target the entire audience obviously

we want to target the entire audience now click on next which is at the bottom right now we need to enter the email subject so this subject is may be what can this be so may be affiliate my email marketing okay email marketing newsletter now preview text preview text is let me show you what a preview text is let me open some mail now as you can see if you see this example element I just got a promotional newsletter from Elementor this is the preview text monthly showcase free templates plugin okay which shows at the preview now when you open this thing this is how it will look and this at the top monthly showcase this whatever the this text is this is the preview text so let's come over here under the preview text I want to enter the same thing now from name again when you come over here as you can see this is the from name Bend from Elementor this will be d from name

so I want this as the from name from email address this is the from email address when you open that mail this email which is shown at the top contact at element or comm this is the from email address okay now we need to do which is one thing click on this next again at the bottom right alright so plain text means very simple plain text no templates no design just text okay so whatever you type you know your for example let me type in hello and let me get some dummy text from the block from this so let me type in this much okay some text so as you can see only text nothing more no design no template nothing is going on over here so this is what plain text means so I'll select this click on next okay now audience is selected subject line preview text everything is fine now let's click just send this thing okay now when you send click on the send now button it will be sent to everyone all your recipients okay so let's click on send now now let me open my mail to show you whether I received this or not and and how does that look okay when I receive it okay now as you can see I received this this is the simple one now the reason

I told you earlier that you should select our email which is a business email is because this when you select a gmail address gmail email it will show this message be careful with this message okay because this as you can see is is sent from real nature at gmail.com but obviously gmail sees that this is not sent by real layer at gmail.com this is sent by some website so whatever your website is for example if you see the Elementor also they are using contact at element or comm so make sure you use something like that okay create a free business email and use that don't use gmail accounts okay that will be much better for you okay so basically you just see that this is how it will look simple plain text okay this is the plain email now let's go to the campaign number two so again I'll click on campaigns now again click on create campaign click on email now this time we have regular email so regular email campaign is just regular email campaign for example if I want to promote my showcase

my latest blogs if I have some news some announcement anything that is just the regular one okay so I'll just and give it a name a regular campaign click on begin now you'll always get same option whom do you want to send this to so address append I want this to send this to this particular group so I'll select this group and if you take Mac this to field personalized to field and select full name okay and click on save so instead of two away instead of two subscriber

it will say to whatever the name is for example I entered my name when I signed up with the newsletter form I entered my name in a year so it will say from whatever the website is to new year so that makes more personalized so select that add a subject line click on add subject and let me just type in subject because this is just for demo purposes preview text subject click on save now you have to select the content so click on design email now just like we created the template earlier you can again create a new template or what you can do you can use this save template okay the latest block template that we have saved select this thing now if you want to do some changes over here you can do that easily and if you are done with everything just click on save and close okay now content is also fine let's go at the bottom and here you have this send either you can send it or you can schedule it if you click on schedule what happens you can suppose I want to deliver this I want to send this tomorrow so I'll select Friday tomorrow or maybe not Friday most every times if you see email marketing or email or email Letta works best on Monday so I'll select 15 and whatever time for example - am i sorry - p.m. not 2 a.m. 2 p.m. 3 p.m. or 11 M whatever time you want to select that click on schedule temp campaign so at that particular time this campaign or this newsletter will be sent

so you can also schedule that if I want to say if you want to send this instantly simply click on send again click on send now and this will be sent instantly now come over here let me show you again okay now as you can see this is how it will look this is the logo this is the name of whatever the name is this this title and everything all this link everything is working over here so this is how the mail will look like and again I am saying use a business email so that you don't get this message if you click on look save that is fine I you won't get that message but the better option is to always use business emails let me cut all these things now now let's see the third style which is the automation which is very very important that will really help you a lot so again click on campaigns

click on create campaign select email now this time select automated now as you can see there are many different things that you can use in automated email your tagged contacts welcome new subscribers see happy birthday share blog updates so here when you select the share blog updates your newsletter recipients will get blog RSS feed update I think the best option to select is this one welcome new subscribers so select this welcome **new subscribers** and you can name it anything so I'm naming it welcome campaign you can select the list so let's select this one click on begin now as you can see or this thing is already designed we have this thing so if you want to design it according to you you can click on design email okay now name your email email subject so maybe not this just type in welcome to our family blocking family whatever you can type in okay from name from email address so instead of this again I am saying just type in some email address if you have created some nassim ill do that okay type in use that for example something like New Year at support at in block to calm add minute block do.com something like that okay click on next now again you can just use any one of these regular campaign save template layouts you I think there is one for welcome as well in this so whatever that a template is for example

I want to use the same template again I can design it again so whenever someone signs up on my website they will receive this template okay I will click on save and continue now you have to change the trigger for example one day after **subscriber** joins your list if you want to change this this click on edit now whenever someone enters the email address and click on sign up you have to decide from that time when should this welcome message or welcome template or campaign should be sent so for example how many times should they wait if you want to send them immediately you can just select immediately and as soon as the person enters their email address click on subscribe to newsletter they will receive this welcome message if you want to wait for some hours for example 1 hour 5 hours 10 hours you can enter that okay so that is what this trigger does for example I am selecting 5 hours click on update trigger so when the person enters that email address after 5 hours they will get this welcome message ok now click on next ok so everything is present audience is selected tracking is selected welcome is also selected now click on start sending ok now

whenever someone selects that email address enter their email address they will get this as the Welcome message after 5 hours ok so this is how this is done now let's again go back to campaigns now let's see what is a be **testing** and how to use that so again click on create campaign email a be test now let's name it anything so I'll just name it a be testing click on begin now let me explain you what this a B testing is ok first of all let's choose the audience I'll select the same audience click on next now this a be testing won't work with this because I have only one subscriber but I'll show you what it is so first of all you have to select what percentage of recipients should receive your test combination make sure to select hundred person that is the best option now what this does is it you can test different combination which performs better for example you have subject line you can max test maximum of three combination in subject line you can add two or three different subjects line

for example one subject line can be how to do email marketing other could be how to earn from email marketing and third subject line could be like how did I on thousand dollars per month from email marketing now what this will do is when you have three different subjects and you have our target audience

for example you have maybe thousand recipients so 333 that is the one-third of thousand they will receive one subject line another 333 will receive another subject line and rest of the people will receive the third subject line oke which means that approximately 300 people will receive the same mail but with a different subject line the another 300 people or one-third people will receive the same mail with a different third with a different subject line and the rest of the people will also receive the same mail same content same thing but this subject line will be different now this is very useful because it will help you to see how your audience is performing if you see you can see the analytics how many people open that how many people read that how many people clicked on some link which was given in the content so you can decide which line which subject line is performing better for you very very important now similarly you can use another one which is from name so this can be an example

for example I can type from mayor shake and another combination can be from technewser so I can see whether people open the mail more when the from name is Nia shake or they when or whether they open the email more when the from name is technewser or some other name okay so that is what it is useful for now if I select from name there are two combinations click on next I'll get an error okay there are no more combination available then recipients so only one person is available and combination is two so let me do one thing now let me cancel this thing me log out from here let me login from my personal account because I in that I have some more you know email addresses

so that I can show you what happens after this now let me use this account let me again do the same things campaign create campaign email or a be test let me name it a be test click on begin choose audience so here as you can see I have around 1600 people so I can select that click on next now I won't get that error for example I want to chew I want to select different from name now as you can see recipient / combination so around 800 people will receive same mail from different person name like Technewser.in and rest 800 people will receive the same email to same content everything same but from different name like Mahesh.com so as I select that click on next and email subject will just type in subject review text subject now as you can see here we have the variation from name one variation can be ponmahesh from email address can be real here another variation can be technewser and email address can be same or different it all depends on you now you will get which variation is performing better when do people click the open the email more or click the link more when a particular name is given now track open track click it will read track how many people opened it

how many people clicked on the link and everything now click on next now again you can select any templates so you can just go ahead and create a new template but will as you can see I have in this account I have few templates created promotion Time black friday' template and all those things so maybe let's select the black friday' template click on next okay as you can see this is a simple template I have a call to action in all those things now click on from before sending obviously I won't be sending it but as you can see everything is proper

now you can just click on send and this will be sent now once it is sent you can check all the results you can come to your website if you want to check the results you can come to your website let's click on campaigns now from here make sure to select the audience first for example what watch we have whichever audience you have sent this to so I am selecting this audience now as you can see I sent this one Black Friday if you want to see the result or report you can click on this link view report now this is how you will see OK 186 people received that and 84 people out of that open that 33 people clicked on some link to people bounced off and one person unsubscribed okay so as you can see all the information is given on this date how many people open on this date how many people opened and clicked on that and what was the time as you can see the I send this on 10:30 a.m. and most of the people opened that at that same time and as you can see the everything is all the links are given and which were the top links that got clicked so this was the top link blocked or calm then Twitter link Facebook link and which I got subscriber which was the subscriber which opened the most so these subscribers opened the most ok so with this and you also have some geographical locations for example top location by open so most of the people from USA opened my email and only 3 from India opened that no worries alright yes so as you can see it is so useful all these data is so useful to see what is performing better ok so this is what a be testing does now let me show you some ecommerce related things

for example if you have an e-commerce website there are few things which will be useful for you so let me first open an e-commerce website let me cut all these things ok so I am using this example now this design is how I created this design in one of my books so if you want to watch ecommerce website you drill that those are also present on my website so first of all let's go to dashboard first thing that we need to do we need to install a new plugin MailChimp for commerce so let's do that how our plugins click add new search for MailChimp for commerce just type in that thing alright so this is the plug-in MailChimp for WooCommerce by mail chimp so click on install now now let's activate this plug-in so click on activate now first of all we need to integrate MailChimp with this plug-in or with this website so for that again we need the API key so I'll click on this click on account now ok under extras you will see API keys click on that copy your API key from here come to your website paste in that link click on save all changes so we have only one option right now connect when we save changes we will get some more options now as you can see another option came store settings so here you have to enter your email address your name your address city code state whatever it is your phone number your location or and currency so make sure to use the currency which you are using on your website for example on your website if you are using USD use USD if you aren't if on your website you are using Indian rupee then select Indian rupee from here now click on Save Changes again when you save changes we'll get third option let's wait now as you can see list of details now default from name whatever default from name you want default email address default subject default language everything click on save all changes now select the list ok

so I am selecting maybe this list list 1 and subscribe to newsletter for opt-in check out so this is very good option which means that whenever a person wants to check out they will get an option we want to subscribe to our newsletter so that is very good so that we can see whenever there is some purchase made by any person they will be automatically subscribed to the newsletter so that we can send them coupons or promotional things ok so opt-in settings as you can see it is selected now make sure this option is selected visible checked by default so by default that thing is checked that the person wants to subscribe to the newsletter if they uncheck that that's fine but by default it is checked now click on save all changes all right now let's see whether this setting is working so let me open this website in a new tab now let's add a product in the card and let's try to checkout let's see whether we get that option or not so let me open this product okay this is a simple product click on **Add to Cart** now let's go to a cart okay

we have this product let me cut this thing now let's click on proceed to checkout scroll down now as you can see your email address whenever the person gives the email address this thing is already tick marks subscribe to our newsletter and this is already tick mark if the person does not UNTAC this they will be subscribed to our newsletter and we can send them you know maybe information related to their order we can send them coupons we can send them promotional emails okay so this is working now let's see how we can send a thank-you mail to person whoever makes the first purchase on our website and let's see or maybe let's see how to send coupons to them for the first purchase okay

so I'll come back oh you click on campaigns and again click on **create campaign email automated** now select ecommerce section now as you can see thank first time customer is given over here select that now select the list which you want to use click on begin ok now as you can see there are three emails which are already selected first one is thank you for your purchase which will be send in a one hour after subscriber purchase anything from your store then after 10 days they will get another mail tell us about your purchase how was your purchase then after 20 days they will get another mail which has all the recommended products for them if you want to trick you change the trigger up after how many days you can obviously change that and for instead of thank you for your purchase if you want to send them some coupons if you want to redesign this you can click on design email and you can click select this the email subject like thank you for your purchase or maybe you can just type in let me first type in this thing maybe you can just type in like this is thank you for your purchase we have a coupon a coupon code for you which you can use for your next purchase okay so when they get a coupon for example if you are getting if you're giving them 10% discount so they're very high chances that to get that 10% discount they may again shop on your website very important option so select all these things click on next now select any layout or create your own layout for example you can just select any simple layout in which you just have maybe this one just select one column let's select this one very simple one because you are just thanking them the first email which you which is for thanking don't try to sell them something that would be really bad so just thank them so again change your logo and everything instead of this text just type in like let's type in the same thing thank you for your purchase if you want to give them some coupon code add that code over here like use this coupon code you will get maybe 20% discount on your next purchase okay and the coupon code is like 20 off okay maybe this is the coupon code and it's in Creole let's make this coupon code bold so select this much select this be it will make it bold and let's change the color to red so that you know it is quite visible now as you can see in the preview this is quite visible now you can change these text let's change that okay so whatever you like it you can click on save and close click on save and continue ok and click on next now we also need to design these two things so you get the idea so again design the second one is the design the template again design the third one click on start sending and it will start sending to people who make purchase on your website okay

so this is how it works so we have seen **how to send thank you for the first purchase** and how to send coupons now let's see the last option obviously there could be more things to show but I think this Time is already getting quite bigger quite lengthier so i want to show you the last thing which is abandoned cart so some sometimes it happens that a person has added a product in the cart but they haven't made the check out for maybe one week two weeks or ten days

so you can send them a message that you know what we have seen that you have this product in your cart do you want to check out or maybe you get I'll we are ready to give you five percent discount if you check out ok so that kind of meal so for that again first of all come back to your website click on campaigns now click on create campaign click on email automated select **ecommerce** and you have this option ton turn on an abandoned card email select that select this store so whatever web side you have connected with this so we have connected this website or technewser store as you can see the name of your website is given over here technewser stores so select that technewser store here it is click on begin now as you can see sent to and if you have you have this trigger technewser store customer six hours after the abandoned item in their cart okay so you can edit recipient and you can change this timing and you have the content over here again go to design email now as you can see we get another option or new option abandoned cart and in that we have or we already have few layouts

so if you want to see that layout how it looks let's see how it will look okay as you can see this is how it will look instead of this it will show you the image of that card which is abandoned the price and they will have this call-to-action returned to check out so they can click on return to checkout and they can do the check out on the website so this is very useful if you want to use this one or whatever design you want to use select that click on change template now if you want to design it more you can you have some more options like you can add some promo code you can add some social share all these options so

for example if you want to add some recommended products as well you can use this one this which product recommended drag and drop it over here okay now as you can see two products are recommended to your blog - number of recommendation if you want to increase this to four products four products will be rec- ommended to them with all the price and everything all the call- to-action and everything click on save and close if you want to give them some promo code you can drop this promo code over here and choose the always try make sure to choose this store if you have connected multiple stores and description let's add the promo code now as you can see this is so very advanced plug-in I

see that because I have don't have any promo code created on my **e-commerce website** I am NOT able to do that so I think this is a very good option if I had created any work promo code on my website under this promo code option I would get that option I could select that and I could use that to promote it if you didn't want to see how to create a promo code you can how our products and you can have a woo commerce and you will see this coupons using this you can create different promo codes and you can select those promo codes over here and click on Save Changes click on save and continue so as you can see everything is happening in a very nice manner in a very professional manner ok and after that again just send it and once you send it everything will start working on your website

so with this we have completed this book I hope this book was helpful I think it should be helpful for you guys I would highly recommend you to start doing email marketing very very useful it you know improves the goodwill of your market people see that you are sending these **automated messages** like you have abandoned your cart do you have recommended products and all these things thanking or may be thanking visitors welcoming visitors or new visitors these things are a thing very nice very important you know it will give you some good will people really like that okay you know what this person really cares about the customer and everything so I think it will really improve the performance and profitability of your website so make sure you use they just don't study the book try to use this try to implement this on your website okay so if you liked this Time make sure to give a thumbs up to this Time subscribe and click on the bell icon on our YouTube channel I will post a video about this email marketing complete guide. so that you don't miss any future updates if you have any doubt any comments any such for me you can leave them in the comments section below thanks a lot & see you in the next one

If any related quries about that pls refer this

https://www.youtube.com/watch?
v=aKrDmHBjRrA&t=8s
https://www.youtube.com/watch?v=dSM9P_jYabU

If   any   doubts   related   this   please   mail   to
`` ` ` ` ` ` ` ` ` ` ` ` ` `` *mahz@groarz.com* `` ` ` ` ` ` ` ` ` ` ` ``

**please give a perfect review about our email marketing
guide before checking the videos.**

*****

www.ingramcontent.com/pod-product-compliance
Lightning Source LLC
Chambersburg PA
CBHW030545220526
45463CB00007B/2986